MW01204736

MISSION POSSIBLE
For Educator's Success

Sly Bell 12/07/2024

Mission Possible
For Educator's Success

SYLVESTER BELL

Staleon Group
Publications
Orlando • Dalla

Also by Sylvester Bell

Dedication

I would like to dedicate this book to Superintendent Sharonica L. Hardin-Bartley and Assistant Superintendent for People and General Administration, Dr. Rebecca O'Connell.

These two ladies are role models to ALL Educators. They have helped me to believe in myself and inspired me to stay focused on my vision. Again, I want to salute these leaders in education with dignity and honor.

- Sylvester Bell

Table Of Contents

From the Author

PRICELESS

Teaching is like a form of Art,
The beauty is for all to see.
A teacher's labor is Priceless,
It brings joy to others and me.

We need to celebrate all Teachers,
And show them we care.
Their legacy lives on,
For the next generation to share.

I wish we had a" Respect Day!"
March would be good to view.
Let's show teachers across the Nation,
We appreciate all they do!

I am aware, teachers have personal lives,
But their love, you can't compare.
One thing our Governors could do,
Is make sure Teacher's
Salaries are Competitive too!

It's just so Amazing,
Teachers train others too!
Such as: Doctors, Nurses,
Lawyers, and Judges,
Just to name a few.

I believe School Districts can do
Better, I know this for a fact.
Teachers are preparing families for the
Future,
So, let's make sure we have
their backs.

Wake up America! Public Education
Must be on the Rise.
We have to solve the teacher
Shortage, If we want our
Country to Survive!

Foreword

by Rebecca C. O'Connell

There is no hiding that being a teacher today has its challenges. When I was a teacher back in the day, the first 45 minutes of happy hour on Fridays was spent with stories from the week. The stories were memorable among my peers and some to this day I remember like they were yesterday. Sylvester Bell has set out to remind and encourage educators with his poetic inspiration just how important and valued you are to the students, families and systems you serve. I never knew my youthful instructional-self would cross paths with Mr. Bell many years later to find he was exactly the way I remembered.

Typically, it is not until many years later you realize the people you touched as educators still hold a small piece of you in their heart. Do you ever wonder what you did or what you said to earn that special space? It was not an amazing lesson you planned or a trip you took them on, it was not a treat or occasion, it was simple, you noticed them. You gave them a moment of yours; it was a look, a hug, an extra ear, a smile, a reference to something they told you, a compliment, you knew their name, you shared a laugh, or a cry, you got excited for them, or checked in knowing something just was a little off. That was the moment you earned a space in their heart, and you would live there forever.

Educators live in the hearts of humans everywhere, and your paths will cross again sooner or later. In an instant the memory of you will be pulled back into their reality. As you go through each day impacting the academic success of your students, remember the greatest impact you will have on them is seeing them as a person.

- Rebecca C. O'Connell, EdD

Mission Possible

For Educator's Success

A SCHOOL'S DELIGHT

School Secretaries are the backbone to every,
school's delight.
They are preparing for Opening Day,
As they welcome back staff on sight.

School Secretaries are the Key,
To help make sure rooms are ready too.
They contribute to setting the tone in their buildings,
Because their job, they Love to do.

Some teachers like to come in early,
Especially those in their prime.
The secretary checks with the Principal,
To find out which days and the times.

They have to get things right,
Because Opening Day, is in view.
Congratulations, to ALL Secretaries,
May "Special Blessings," always cover you!

*****

A MOTHER'S SUPPORT

What can I say about my Mom,
Who is always in my view?
She helped me stay on task.
I know this is true.

I had a Passion for teaching,
And I retired after thirty years.

My mother kept me encouraged,
Not to walk or live in fear.

Sometimes, I got discouraged,
Just didn't know what to say.
My mother was right there,
To pray with me each day.

There were many Challenges,
Working and going to school, too.
She kept telling me,
"Teaching" is, your Gift to do!

My Mom's Legacy is there,
And that's a Beautiful thing.
Help me Celebrate her Love,
And why she will always be, "My Queen!"

*****

A NURSE'S ROLE

Nurses play a very important role in our schools,
Working to keep students from sickness and pain.
Some students are on medication,
And the nurse remembers their name.

Nurses are highly trained,
To help students understand the way,
Let's be Thankful for Nurses and celebrate them each day.

*****

STAND YOUR GROUND

Teachers, you have to stand your ground,
No matter what comes your way.
When students are having a difficult day,
Don't just turn and walk away.

It's always good to address issues
When things seem to be in despair.
If you want a Productive Classroom,
Be sure to handle the problems with care.

*****

PRINCIPALS SET THE TONE

Principals are a Big Key to success,
They really set the tone.
It's good when they are visible,
And encouraging students to do no wrong.

When Principals greet the students,
It gives them a Thrill.
Helps Scholars to do right,
Regardless of how they feel.

Morning announcements are informing,
Made known to everyone, the expectations for the day.
Such a pleasure to have the Principal,
Come by and check your way.

Principals, are very encouraging,
When Educators know, you have their backs,

They are looking for Support and Guidance,
So they can remain on track.

Educators, it's a blessing to have a Principal
Who is not ashamed to show Love and Care.
It makes your job more enjoyable,
Gives you another reason for why you are there.

*****

PRINCIPAL WITH INTEGRITY

Mr. Triplett is an awesome Principal,
Certainly, this is true.
He looks for us to walk with Integrity,
It's what he expects us to do.
If you want to get him a gift,
Make sure the color is red.
Let's Celebrate our Phenomenal Principal,
Who also wears outstanding threads.

*****

TEACHER OF THE YEAR

Teacher of the year, is a "Great Honor."
It's something that should never be underscored.
All your hard work and labor,
Is not in vain, but will be remembered forever more!

It encourages you to press on,
Your occupation is always in demand.
Continue to Aim for "Greatness"

And expect to keep making huge gains.

*****

SCHOOL LIBRARIANS

School Librarians are so important,
They are a big part of the educational team.
Librarians organize so many things,
that help students focus on their dreams.

They have skills that make reading exciting,
And sometimes, they have productions too.
We should respect and honor our Librarians,
Because they have a lot of work to do.

*****

SCHOOL COUNSELORS

School Counselors have a gift,
It's to spread Love to all man-kind.
They have a lot of knowledge on how to handle problems,
And it helps ease disturbing minds.

Students are allowed to release stress,
Instead of walking around in despair.
Counselors will give you advice,
So your problems, you will be able to bear.

*****

SOCIAL WORKERS

I would like to, and please help me,
"Salute Social Workers,"
Who really are second to None.
Sometimes they work around the clock,
Trying to make sure things get done.

They have so much Compassion for families,
You and I know, their Love is right there.
So, let us Salute ALL Social Workers,
For all the things they do and the time they share.

*****

CUSTODIAN SUPPORT

I give special thanks to custodians,
The work they do each day.
Schools are kept clean,
Which makes the environment pleasant to stay.

Custodians' job are not easy,
They are on call twenty/ four seven,
If you are a custodian,
We salute you ALL forever!

*****

BEFORE AND AFTER CARE

Oh my! parents are real excited,
To have before and after care.
I think parents are grateful too,
Because it's a place for their children to be safe and be
there.

Let's shout out to these workers,
Who take care of our children with such integrity,
This is a "Wonderful Program,"
It helps students learn,
to walk with Dignity.

*****

GRADUATION HONOR

Educators, you should feel very proud,
You have helped students achieve their goals,
Just think how many lives you have changed.
And all the stories they've
shared and told.

I know you have spent, without even counting,
many, many hours,
Preparing lessons and tests.
Now, I'm giving you your well- deserved flowers,
For You have done "Your Very Best!"

*****

MALE TEACHERS

Educators, it's essential that we recruit Male Teachers,
Especially in our Elementary Schools.
This will not only be very powerful,
I believe students will agree:
It's really, really cool.

They can become Role Models,
For students, as time goes on.
It might help parents to keep on pressing,
Without getting mentally stressed or torn.

*****

BUMP ON YOUR JOURNEY

Teachers, there will be bumps on your journey,
I know this is true.
Make sure you walk with dignity,
So you won't lose your passion too.

This journey is not going to be easy,
No shape form or fashion.
Please maintain your love for teaching,
Because I believe you have compassion!

*****

SCHOOL SAFETY

School safely is a concern,
All students should be safe.
If you see a student who seems depressed,
Reach out to them regardless of their race.

Teachers, it's important to know where students are,
Especially through-out the school day.
You must give an account,
Is the only effective way.

*****

SALUTE ALL TEACHERS

Teachers are the reason,
Students smile every day.
You are making a difference,
Teaching them new ways.

It's good to Salute All Teachers,
For their job is never done.
Continue to Support All Educators,
Because they are solely, the ones.

*****

WORK TO DO

Teaching might seem hard,
But that is okay.
You know, you have work to do,

So stay focused on your journey each day.
No, don't get side tracked,
By what students say or do.
You have the gift to teach,
Believe it: this is true.

*****

AN ANGRY STUDENT

A student might be angry,
Before the sun even rises.
If they bring that attitude in the room,
It just might be the reason, why other behaviors arise.

It's good to have a plan,
That will help students keep their Composure.
Give the angry student a job to do.
It could very well bring the negative behavior to closure.

*****

A GREAT TEACHER

If you want to be a Great Teacher,
Keep your eyes on the prize.
Disconnect from Negative People,
Who don't want to see you Rise!

You have so much to offer,
The things you teach and share.
When you have a passion to teach,
Love, will always be there!

*****

DON'T SWEAT

Educators, never allow your
Students to see you Sweat,
Oh, they will try to break you
down.
Hold on to your profession,
And don't forget: you wear the
Crown.

Educators, keep your composure,
Integrity, you must Maintain.
You are a Role Model for your
students,
And kindness is surely good to
Maintain.

*****

EDUCATOR'S SUCCESS

Mission Possible for Educator's Success
is the theme for this season.
We will stand together in Unity,
And help our students to
Achieve.

We are on the same team,
Working to support one another.
Teachers, stay on this journey,
Until ALL is said and done!

*****

PARENTS INVOLVEMENT (Part 1)

Parents involvement is the key
For ALL Educators Success.
When parents are totally involved,
Students will have no choice,
but to do their Best.

Parents can set the tone,
With a loving start of a
student's day.
We celebrate our parents,
Without them student's will
go astray.

I can only imagine,
the things parents go through.
Keep in touch with your
children 's teachers,
It's an awesome thing to do.

*****

PARENTS INVOLVEMENT (Part 2)

I know we have parents,
Who would like to see their child's progress.
Since they are committed to the course,
There is no time for them to
Stress.

I wish we could go back,
To the time when parents had an educational view.
They would stop by the classroom,
Which served as a "Pop Up"
Observation, too.

Parents get Excited,
About things students have
done.
I'm grateful to All parents,
Because they are the only ones!

*****

PARENTS INVOLVEMENT (Part 3)

Parents, you do have a voice,
And it's important to use your words.
Continue to support your child's teachers,
and don't walk around disturbed.

I hope you understand,
Love is always here to repair.
We want to Celebrate All
Parents,
Because your Legacy will
remain there.

*****

PARENTS HELP

Parents, teachers can't make it

Without your help.
That's why we need you, the
Most.
Will you please develop a
check-in-time,
Where student grades will be
on Post?

It will help behavior,
And keep students on
their toes.
Students won't know your
check-in-time,
So let's try it and see how it
Goes.

I think this is a great plan,
Also a way to get parents
Involved.
Each week, the teachers will
receive a call, text message,
or note,
Now, watch problems start
getting solved!

*****

PARENTS HAVE THE POWER

Parents, you have the power,
to make things come into play.
Why not check with your child's teacher,
Actually, you can start today.

I know it can be Overwhelming,
But an action must be in place.
Sometimes a classroom visit,
Will put a smile on the teacher's face.

Parents and Teachers have a job,
Work together to keep things in order.
Let's Model: "Working Together,"
So teachers' jobs will not be so hard.

*****

SPECIALISTS TEACHERS

I can't leave out our Specialist Teachers,
I know this is a fact.
They provide extremely thorough lessons,

That help students achieve their goals, too.
We should never take our Specialists Teachers for granted,
Together with classroom teachers, they make holistic
breakthroughs.

So, please help me salute our "Specialists Teachers" for all
the things they have to do.

*****

GOOD OLD DAYS

Everyday is not the same,
This we know is true.
Grade levels use to go from
Kindergarten to eighth
Maybe that is something
we should go back to.

Sometimes I have to wonder,
Should schools go back
to the Old Way?
Doing whatever helped
our students Grow,
It would be a Great Big Plus,
Today.

*****

KEEP ON REACHING

Teachers, take time to reflect
On your style of teaching,
And Focus on how to help,
Students keep on reaching.

Students need to pay attention
To lessons taught.
Teachers continue to stand,
And let out a "Big Victory" Shout!
*****

STORY TIME

Educators, Story Time is
always a Plus,
It teaches students to listen
and learn about plots,
characters, settings and problems.
I encourage all of you to have
Story Time, and even, Make
it a Must!

You can be creative and
make up a story,
or just read books
from your Reading Inventory.

*****

THE CHOICE IS YOURS

It's an honor to become a teacher,
The choice is truly in your heart.
You decided to pursue your dream.
So, let nothing pull you apart!

It takes a Special Person
to be a teacher
Love must always be there.
What an opportunity to teach,
It allows you to talk, love, and share!

*****

STAY CALM

Educators, you must stay calm
If not, things can get out of
Control.
Students may come to class,
And continue to make some
Noise.

Sometimes you might not
Understand,
Why students act the way
they do.
If you remain calm,
Victory is in it for You!!!

*****

ROTATING CLASSES

Middle School is very fast paced,
Students are Exchanging
classes each day.
They have about three minutes,
to report to each class that day.

Some students may detour in the hall,
And decide to come to class late.
They will need to get a hall pass,
So they will not be marked absent
that day.

*****

GREAT JOB

Middle School Educators are
doing an amazing job,
Getting students ready for
High School.
Students are faced with many
Challenges, and some of
them just want to act "Cool."

The big concern in Middle School,
Is students are fighting each other.
I salute all teachers and School Counselors,
For encouraging students to
Respect one another.

*****

MIDDLE SCHOOL TEACHERS

Now, I have Encouraging Words,
They are for all Middle School Teachers.
Your labor is not and has not been in
Vain, continue to press forward and
Maintain.

Middle School teachers are
Working hard,
To prepare our Students for Success.
Your Faithful Dedication
Is why you ALL are the Best!

*****

SUMMER SCHOOL

I have good news for Educators.
If you need to pay some bills,
You may apply for Summer School.
Mighty nice resources, for real.

Summer School is about a four
week program,
It's to enrich students' skills.
Such an opportunity to gain
Knowledge, and it should give
everyone involved a thrill!

*****

NEW TEACHERS

The first semester is on the Horizon,
School is about to start.
Get ready to receive your Scholars,
And let "Love " flow from your Heart.

Teachers, if this is your First Year, Congratulations,
Your Choice is Smart.
You are on your way to Excellence,
If you "Never Let the Passion Depart!"

*****

STAY IN THE FIGHT

I hope these Inspirational
Messages are Encouraging,
You to stay in the fight.
Indeed, we shall overcome,
Keep the faith, and continue to do
what's right.

I know it seems like a long journey,
But you can get through it.
Excellence is the key to success,
So, no need to walk around
Mentally Stressed!

*****

DREAM JOB

Do you know your gift,
The things you like to do?
Once you fine your dream job,
See it and bring it forth in your
View.

I wanted to be a teacher,
From the time I turned sixteen
I have taught thirty years,
And I've never walked in fear.

*****

PARENTS AS TEACHERS

Help me Salute Teachers,
Who sometimes have children too.
They are constantly giving instructions,
Which seems to them a joy to do.

Teaching begins at home
Certainly, this is a fact.
If you are a parent and teaching school,
give yourself a pat on the back!

*****

ONE AND ONLY

I want teachers to stay
Encouraged,
For all the things you
have already done.

Without a doubt, I know
for sure,
Teachers are Second to
None!

Teaching is a Wonderful
Profession,
It's a job one can Adore.
There is always room for
Improvement,
So, keep growing and
continue to learn more.

*****

TIME TABLES LEARN

If students are struggling in math,
We need to help get the problem
Solved
Students must learn their
Multiplication Facts,
So, come on, let's get every
One involved!

Educators, homework will
be a good place to start.
Have the facts recited at Night
To check for Understanding,
Make sure students know,
the ones that were right!

*****

SENTENCE DICTATION

I remember Sentence Dictation,
Back in the day.
Students would take a test
Weekly, and we learned to
spell the right way.

Just maybe, we need to revisit this Strategy
Though I know it's not in style.
My suggestion is gives students the test,
As you, teacher walk the aisle.

*****

STANDARDS

Educators must set the standards,
For the students in their class.
They have High Expectations,
It's the reason they will last.

A rubric score is used,
So students don't have to ponder.
The goal is to score a three
or four, and no one has to wonder.

*****

CELEBRATE TEACHERS

A teacher's job is never done.
There's so much work to do.
We must Celebrate our Teachers,
They are Role Models for others, too.

*****

BEST OCCUPATION (Part 1)

There are three factors
Why Teaching is the Best
"Occupation":

Teachers have Vacation,
Holidays, and Personal Days,

throughout the year.
In September, there is Labor Day,
A good time to Reflect and
Celebrate with Cheer.

October, is not too bad,
Homecoming is right there.
This is a time
to enjoy Football games
and come together and
Share!

*****

BEST OCCUPATION (Part 2)

November is my favorite Month,
Let me explain Why,
My Birthday is November 3rd,
It's also a Month of
Thanksgiving and I am so
Thankful, that's is no lie!

When I was Teacher,
I took November and December
too.
Enjoy all the Holidays
and the many things you can
Do!

*****

BEST OCCUPATION (Part 3)

Educators, I want you to get Excited,
Yes, Vacation time is in your View.
And because you are an Educator,
Please plan to Enjoy your
Vacation time Too!

*****

BEST OCCUPATION (Part 4)

Please understand the advantages of Becoming a Teacher,
Heads up: Another day off in January,
Thanks to Dr. King, who was a Civil
Rights Preacher.

February is a short month,
Yet, another Holiday to Behold.
Just look at all the holidays,
That give Educators more reasons
For hope and a job to adore.

*****

BEST OCCUPATION (Part 5)

Springtime is in the atmosphere.
For some, it the best time of the year.
I have good News to tell you,
Spring Vacation is Near,
Thanks to your Career!

Now, come the month of April,
No vacation but no need to
Pout.
Keep Your eye on the prize,
School is almost out!

*****

CLASS MEETINGS

Educators, I want to encourage you
to start having Class Meetings.
A good time might be after lunch,
This could be the best time,
Because it's when problems occur so much.

Class meetings can solve many problems
Before they get out of hand.
This could be a good strategy
To use, and I believe, it will be an Excellent Plan

*****

MEMORY LANE

Do you Remember when
There were neighborhood Schools?
Student's had to walk to school,
Regardless of rain, snow or
if the weather was just cool.

I grew up in the projects,
And it was no joke.

My books were carried in my
hand,
Then I placed them inside
my coat.

Teachers had Resources,
And they did not play at all.
There were no issues of
students being in the hall.

We learned our vocabulary words,
Did it, using the radio too,
Monday, Wednesday, and Friday,
They told the teachers what
to do.

Parents were totally involved,
With subjects taught in class,
They always checked with
the teachers,
To make sure students were
going to pass.

I know things have changed from,
The way students behaved in the past.
We, as Educators,
need parents help to check with
Their child's teacher,
They will do the Right thing
and Pass!

*****

STUDENT'S REST

It is very important,
For students to get plenty
of rest.
They need to go to bed early,
So each morning, they
are at their Best!

I believe part of their behavior
problems, due to students
not getting enough sleep.
Let's mention this to their parents,
Giving them an opportunity to
Speak.

*****

GRADE BOOK

Do you remember back in the day,
When teachers used a grade book?
Every week teachers would
give a test,
And students were trained to
"Look."

Math, Reading,
Spelling and Language Arts,
just to name a few,
The Data was there for
teachers to see,
In case students needed to Review.

*****

TEACHER'S FAVORITE

There are some students
You can depend on,
They have your backs, it's true.
Always trying to do things
That are pleasing,
Because they are looking up
to You!

*****

BULLY IN THE CLASSROOM

Teachers must not allow
This behavior to Continue,
Especially if it's taking place in the classroom.
A child should have the right
to speak, Morning, Recess, or Noon.

Bullying is an Awful thing,
And should Absolutely, not
be Tolerated at ALL!
Please stay Alert and on
the look out,
And always, be Prepared to
answer the call!

*****

SCHOOL'S OPENING DAY

School's opening day,
can be Overwhelming,
There is excitement in the air.
Teachers are prepared to
show students,
The reason why they care.

The students have their supplies,
Book-bags, pens, and paper, too.
It's nothing like Opening Day,
Students are prepared when
they walk through!

*****

KEEP THE LOVE

Educators, you have come this
far by Faith, to lead our
students to their success.
Mission is Possible for ALL,
And don't even entertain
giving up to Stress.
Educators are Amazing,
With all the things you say and do.
Educators, you must Embark upon Victory,
And Embrace the student's Love too!

*****

CONFIDENCE

Do you want to be a Successful Teacher?
Building Confidence must be there.
Never let fear or doubt enter,
Hindering you until you feel, You can't share.

Your Principal, expects nothing less,
So give him or her your best.
Have Confidence and observe,
how you will pass your Tests!

*****

TEAM MEETINGS

Team meetings are required,
And they can Support Growth.
It's a time to share ideas,
And learn how lessons should flow.

All teachers are not the same,
This is a known fact.
When having team meetings,
Make sure you have each
other's back.

*****

ARRIVE EARLY

Time controls our lives,
Everywhere we go.
If your work schedule
starts at 8, I recommend
arriving at 7:30 or so.

When you get to work early,
It helps put your mind at ease.
You have time to relax and
collect your thoughts,
So expect your day to be a Breeze!

*****

OBSERVATIONS

Teachers, you will have observations,
However, don't allow this to
Stress you out.
Always state your objective,
So students know what the lesson is about

I would like to suggest to you:
To let students pull their own weight,
When it comes to observations,
Have students in groups with
other classmates.

*****

DATA DRIVEN

As a teacher, you must keep up
with Data,
And I know this is No Lie.
You work in Data Driven Districts,
To monitor Progress on a Fly.

You are to meet the needs of
each student,
Regardless if they are on
grade level or not.
Share information with Parents,
So there will be no need to stir the pot.

*****

REPORT CARDS

This is a Special Time of the year,
Allows everyone to see the Progress
students have made.
We should have Conferences with Parents,
To see if lesson was left Undone.

I suggest: Don't wait to the very end.
If a student is
not making any progress at all,
Let the Parents Know,
Do it with a note or a phone call.

*****

JOURNAL WRITING

Journal writing sets the tone
to start your day with a bang.
When students enter the room,
Start with writing and help them
Maintain.

The topic will be on the board,
to help them get started.
It's uplifting watch them write,
as the passion pours from their
hearts.

*****

ESTABLISH A ROUTINE

All teachers need to establish a Routine.
It can help classroom morale.
Students can enter the room,
standing tall and walking with Style.

Students need a good breakfast,
To start their day with class.
Having a Routine
Will enable Students to last.

*****

PAY DAY

Pay day is so Encouraging,
When it comes into play.
After all your Hard Work,
It inspires teachers to stay.

I know teachers have responsibilities,
Things they need to get done.
Let's celebrate our Educators,
They are: Second to None!

*****

TEACHER'S GOAL

Every teacher has a Goal,
I know this for a fact.
When you establish a
good rapport with students,
I promise, they will have your back.

It is often very Challenging,
As you continue to meet your goal.
Let Nothing stop your PROGRESS,
And watch how Growth unfolds.

*****

THE BIG PICTURE

Teachers, I to Encourage you ALL,
Our students need our Special Touch.
Yes, it can be Overwhelming,
But tell students You Love them Much.

Let's look at the Big Picture,
See who they can become down the road,
It's a Great feeling,
You helped them bear their
load.

*****

INTEGRITY

There will be situations,
That arise every now and then.
So, maintain your Integrity,
It will help you until the end.

*****

POST RULES

Classroom Rules need to be Posted,
It helps students to Remain Focused.
I believe when they see the Rules,
Your Classroom will not be in a Commotion.

Every day, go over the rules,
You are Establishing the room's

Foundation.
When students read and learn the Rules,
They will also know your Expectations!

*****

HOMEWORK CHECK

Homework has a purpose,
It's for every student to do.
Gives students time to review,
What they learned today, too.

A good time to Check Homework,
Is when students enter the class.
This is a Wonderful Resource,
It helps students want to pass!

*****

NO AUDIENCE

Educators, here is a suggestion:
When a student is out of control,
Take the student to the side,
Have the student write their Goal.

It's important to keep a calm voice.
Yelling and Screaming will
not do it.
If you try this Strategy,
I promise, You will remain Legit.

*****

HANDLE STRESS

Have you ever been Stressed Out
Trying to teach a lesson?
Students are being Disrespectful
Instead of Respectful.

You might have to count to five,
To get Everyone back on track.
Just Relax an Don't let stress,
Have Your blood pressure,
All out of Wack!

*****

SOCIAL MEDIA

Social Media can be a major problem,
And cause trouble in various schools.
Students will bring their issues to class,
And walk around trying to look, "Cool."

Students are disrespecting each other,
Because of things they see on Facebook.
Please Encourage Students:
"Don't bring Social Media
issues in the "Classroom,"
There is No need for others
to take a look.

*****

HIGH EXPECATIONS

Teachers have High Expectations,
It is for all students to succeed..
We have buried the Word,
"Can't,"
Now, each student may proceed.

We need to keep that Energy,
Knowing each student can Excel.
Remember: Have High Expectations,
Expect All Students to Prevail.

*****

SUCCESS

It takes time to become successful,
So please, don't act surprised.
Continue to be Faithful,
And watch how you Rise.

We all should have Goals,
Believe you will Achieve.
Teachers, stay Strong,
And Observe how you will
Receive.

*****

TOTAL ENCOURAGEMENT

What should you do when a
student pass a test?
Make sure you
give them an Encouraging Word.
Help students learn
It's important to always do their Best.

When students are doing the
right thing,
What should the teacher do?
Praise and Encourage Them,
To students, this will mean,
"Everything!"

*****

ABSENT DAY

Teachers, sometimes you will be Absent,
One day or maybe two.
Make sure you leave
Grade Level Appropriate Work,
And not "Just Busy" Assignments to do.

When you leave "Detailed" Plans,
That is really" Great!
Remember: the Goal is for students to continue to
LEARN,
And not Just "Associate."

*****

CLASSROOM ENVIRONMENT

It's important to have a
Decorative Classroom,
So when students walk
through the door,
They will feel "Welcomed!"
Because their classroom, is
the one for all to Adore!

I recommend you have
Centers, such as: Math,
Reading and Writing too.
Having an attractive room,
will stir up your students, excitement
When it's yours and their room,
They have in their View!

*****

SAVE THE DATES

Teachers, it's good to keep a Calendar,
Mounted on your refrigerator door.
It will help you organize those
Dates, you can't Ignore.

Also, you can mark your Paydays.
A calendar will help you keep
Things intact,
So, start marking down your dates,
To remind and keep you on track.

*****

KEEP YOUR SMILE

Every day is not the same,
Certainly, this is true.
When you arrive in your classroom,
Make sure, you keep your
"Smile," Too.

Make sure you have a "Do Now"
That promotes an Attitude
"To Work."
Let your smile
Encourage students,
Not to act like a jerk.

*****

MEMORABLE SCHOOL YEAR

Have a memorable School Year,
Is what I want to say.
Keep your eyes on the prize,
Until the month of May.

You are the captain of your ship,
And let your story be told.
Expect great things this school year,
And watch how things unfold!

*****

TEACHERS MUST PRESS

Support Staff Must Press
Support Staff must press on,
Regardless how they feel.
I know sometimes it's overwhelming,
Make sure you keep your zeal.

*****

TEACHER LESSONS

Teachers have a Plan,
To be followed Every day.
Objectives must be met,
As lessons are prepared for the day.

When presenting your lesson,
Make sure the students are Engaged.
This is Key to Their Success,
Helps keep behaviors from becoming Outraged.

*****

TEACHERS AS PARENTS

Teachers acting as parents,
Must show Love, Tenderness, and Care.
We have a Responsibility,
To lead, guide and share.

There are times when we have to correct,
It helps students

stay on the right track.
Teachers must stand together,
And show, we have student's backs.

*****

SUCCESSFUL TEACHERS

There are three Important things, to become a Successful
Teacher!

Classroom Management,
Passion for students and
Understanding the Curriculum.

Reading the Quotes, hopefully, will encourage
you to become A Successful
Teachers!

My brother and sister Teachers,
Your journey is about to start.
Welcome to a New School Year,
Always keep Love in your heart!

*****

SUPPORT STAFF

I would like to acknowledge our support staff,
They have an important role in our schools.
Support staff work with students who have "Special
Needs,"

Assisting them with following the rules.
I know, sometimes, you feel overwhelmed,
But, your work is not in vain.
Continue to make Great strides,
And watch how much they Gain!

*****

A TEACHER RESPONSIBILITY

A Teacher has a
Great Responsibility,
That money can't Buy.
I promise you,
"This is No Lie."

Teachers have to
be totally Committed,
Every second,
minute, and hour.
Continue to share your knowledge,
And do it with Integrity and
Power!

*****

SUBSTITUE TEACHERS

Substitute Teachers, I want to encourage you,
You are an important part of the teaching team.
When you receive your assignment,
Just think of the many strategies you bring.

It's always good to arrive early,
With the plans there, in your view.
You will need confidence, also,
To perform the tasks entrusted to you!

Be assured, the students will put you to the test,
Beginning when they arrive at the door.
Remember, you set the tone,
When their feet touch the Classroom floor.

You establish the Classroom rules,
Make sure the students know,
"It is not a day to play."
Be sure you remain pleasantly firm,

While developing a "Rapport," right away.
Don't see a lesson plan?
Please, don't let this take you out of your lane.
Give the students a writing assignment,
Will help you, the class to maintain.

One key to being successful:
Have students remain in their seats.
You, must be totally engaged.
Watch your day be Good and Sweet!

*****

Special Thanks

Mission Possible for Educator's Success.
We must stand together with Zeal and Zest.

I want to thank All superintendents, especially Dr. Sharonica L. Hardin-Bartley, the commander in Chief of the University City School District, Teacher's, and Parents, for your Love and Support.

I believe this book will inspire ALL Educators across America!

This is your Resource to help ALL to survive in the school Environment.

We shall OVERCOME!

If you need additional Information, please feel free to email me:

Sylvester8323@gmail .com or Sbell@ucityschools.org

- Sylvester Bell

Staleon Group
Publications